"Who," said the owl.

"Who pollinates the flowers

and fruits from the tree?"

"Not I," said the fly.

"It's me," said the bee.

Poppies are nectar-free

but their pollen is divine.

Sweet nectar from the
columbine is shrine

for butterflies

and bees.

But did you know?

Bees also pollinate flowers

on fruits and veggies too...

Without them, there would be no "me" or "you".

So, think about this

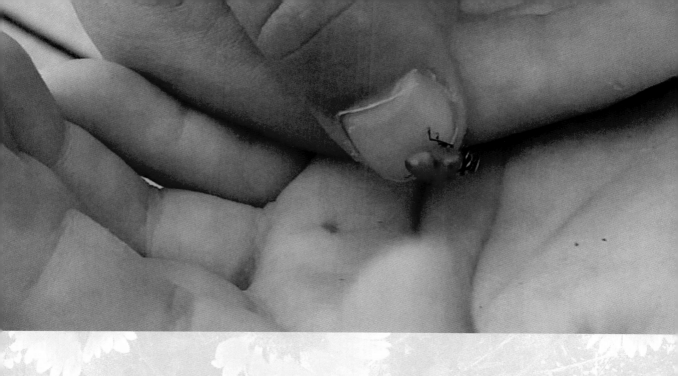

before you squish

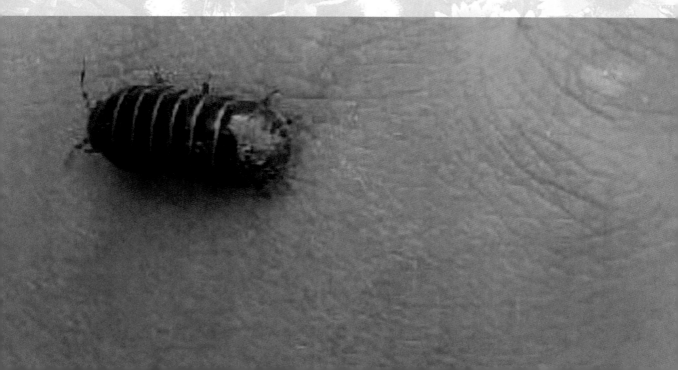

any living thing on land

or in the sea...

Made in the USA
Middletown, DE
10 May 2021